Shakespeare's Britain

Jonathan Bate and Dora Thornton

with Becky Allen

THE BRITISH MUSEUM PRESS

© 2012 The Trustees of the British Museum

Jonathan Bate, Dora Thornton and Becky Allen have asserted
their rights to be identified as the authors of this work.

First published in 2012 by The British Museum Press
A division of The British Museum Company Ltd
38 Russell Square, London WC1B 3QQ

britishmuseum.org/publishing

A catalogue reference for this book is available from the British Library

ISBN 978-0-7141-2826-9

Designed by Will Webb Design
Printed in China by C&C Offset Printing Co. Ltd.

Many of the objects illustrated in this book are from the collection
of the British Museum. Their museum registration numbers are listed
on pages 93–5. Further information about the Museum and its collection
can be found at britishmuseum.org.

Pages 6–7: London (*The Long View*), detail
Wenceslaus Hollar, Amsterdam, 1647
Etching on paper comprising four sheets, H 47.1 cm, W 158.7 cm
British Museum, London

Contents

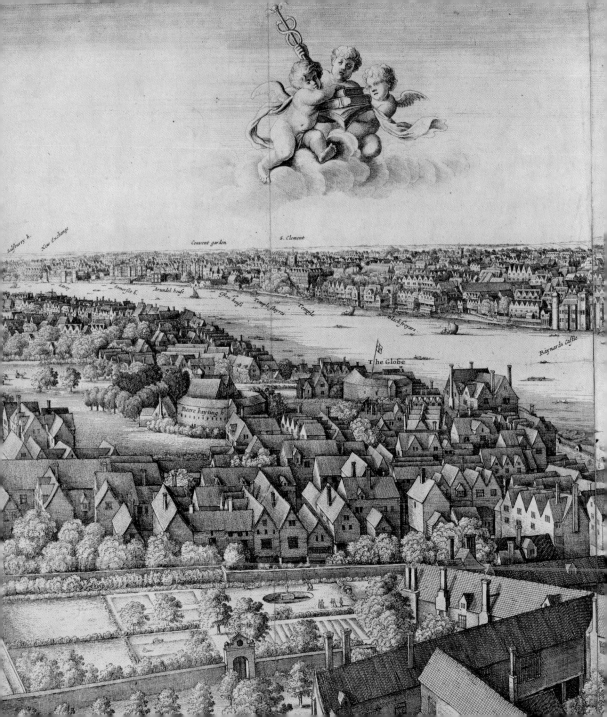

Salisbury h.   New Exchange   Covent garden   S. Clement

Savoy   Somerset h.   Arundel house   Glee house   Temple stayres   Temple   Blackfryars   Baynards Castle

The Globe

Beere bayting h.

S. Pauwls Church

S. ye Waterhouse

S. Andre in Holborne

Heygat

Paulus wharfe

Queene hythe

The 3. Cranes

Stilia

the Eel Ships

THAME

Winchester house

Introduction

WILLIAM SHAKESPEARE (1564–1616) lived in a time of extraordinary change. People's eyes were being opened to new worlds all around them: new global networks of trade and plunder, a new understanding of the cosmos that questioned the old certainty that the earth was the centre of the universe, a new historical consciousness of the past, a new social and ethnic mix in the rapidly expanding city of London, the new spiritual dispensation known as Protestantism, a new sense of what it meant to be English and then to be British.

Within three short generations, the Shakespeare family trod the path from old traditions rooted in feudalism to new forms of entrepreneurship and innovation that are recognizably modern. Richard Shakespeare, William's grandfather, lived in the first half of the sixteenth century. He was a tenant farmer from the village of Snitterfield in Warwickshire. Archival records place him firmly in the context of rural English life of a kind unchanged since early medieval times: fined two pence for not attending the manor court, charged with overburdening the commons with his cattle, fined again for neglecting to yoke his swine. He would rarely have left his village, never have left his county, known little of his nation or the world.

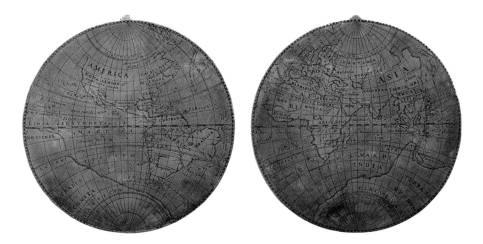

John Shakespeare, Richard's son, made the move from village to town and from farming to shopkeeping. He set himself up as a glover in the nearby market town of Stratford-upon-Avon and carried out a variety of other business ventures on the side. He became a respectable burgher, active in local government. He put his eldest son William, who was born in April 1564, through the admirable local grammar school, from where there was a good chance of going on to university and thence into one of the professions. But then John overstretched himself, taking on mortgages and loans that proved beyond his means to repay. The family fortunes contracted and William was taken out of school. While some of his contemporaries went up to Oxford University, he was left helping out in his father's shop. But then in the late 1580s, now married to Anne Hathaway and with a young family of his own, he made a defining and very modern move: to the city, to London, the capital of the nation and the gateway to the world.

William Shakespeare was fortunate in his timing. He arrived in London at a time of new national confidence. In 1581, Francis Drake had returned from his circumnavigation of the Globe, his ship laden with Spanish gold. In 1588 the Armada was defeated.

The economy was booming and new enterprises were emerging, among them an entirely new phenomenon: the professional entertainment industry. Purpose-built playhouses were springing up in the suburbs to the east of the city and on the south bank of the river Thames – the Theatre, the Rose, the Swan, and in 1599 the best of them all, the Globe.

He began as a bit-part actor, then took to improving the scripts in his company's repertoire, then wrote entire new plays, showing himself equally adept in war-fuelled historical drama, tragedy of blood and helter-skelter comedy. Shakespeare proved himself a more able businessman than his father: most writers for the stage were paid on a piecework basis, a few shillings at a time. But he and his fellow actors made the innovation of forming a joint stock company, taking ownership of their own theatre and sharing the box-office profits. By the early 1600s, William had become a wealthy man – probably the first Englishman in history to make a serious living by his pen – and the owner of a large house back in his home town of Stratford-upon-Avon.

His plays appealed to all classes: the 'groundlings' who paid a penny to stand in the yard and gape in wonder at the kings, clowns and warriors, at the rich costumes and spectacular stage-effects; the clever lawyers and gentlemen about town who appreciated the dazzling verbal artistry of Shakespeare's poetry and prose; and the royal court, for whom command performances were played on festive occasions. Queen Elizabeth herself, and then her successor King James, had a profound understanding of the role of theatre and spectacle in the making of royal power and the formation of a new national self-image.

For Elizabeth I, the nation in question was England. Wales had been formally subsumed by her father Henry VIII, while Scotland was a kingdom of its own. Ireland was a problem, and the cause of bitter division in the final years of the old queen's reign. When she died, unmarried, in 1603, her nephew King James VI of Scotland succeeded to the English throne, as King James I of England. He thus considered himself the King of Britain. When writing

Mr. WILIAM
SHAKESPEARES
COMEDIES
HISTORIES, &
TRAGEDIES,

Published according to the True Originall Copies.

Martin Droeshout sculpsit London.

LONDON

Printed by Isaac Iaggard, and Ed. Blount. 1623.

THE FAMILY OF HENRY VIII:
AN ALLEGORY OF THE TUDOR
SUCCESSION
Lucas de Heere, *c.* 1572
Oil on panel, H 131.2 cm, W 184 cm
National Museum of Wales, Cardiff

historical dramas during the reign of Elizabeth, Shakespeare concerned himself with the English past ('Cry, 'God for Harry, England and Saint George!'"). Once James was on the throne and Shakespeare's acting company was given the title The King's Men, the playwright turned his attention to Scottish (*Macbeth*) and then distinctively British matter (*King Lear* and *Cymbeline King of Britain*).

John Shakespeare had been born shortly before one of the great cataclysms in English history: Henry VIII's break from the universal Roman Catholic church. In the turbulent 1540s and 1550s, the national religion veered from extreme Protestantism in the reign of the boy king Edward VI to a return to Catholicism under Queen Mary. By the time William was born to John and his wife Mary Arden, Queen Elizabeth was on the throne and two key pieces of legislation had come into effect: the 1559 Act of Supremacy re-established the Church of England's independence from Rome, with Parliament conferring on Elizabeth the title Supreme Governor of the Church of England, while the Act of Uniformity, passed the same year, set out the form the English church would now take, including the establishment of the Book of Common Prayer. The diplomatic skill of the Queen and the English gift for compromise had established what historians call the 'Anglican settlement', a middle way between the Catholicism of Rome and the radical Protestantism of Geneva.

But the break from Rome meant that the history and values of the nation had to be rewritten. The London theatre played a huge part in this. By dramatizing the national story and by investigating the great political questions of the day – good government and bad, tyranny and rebellion, assassination and civil war – Shakespeare gave his people, and London's visitors from around the world, a vocabulary and a vision with which they could explore who they were and what it meant to be English, British, or indeed to be a citizen of the world.

World City

'I hope to see London once ere I die'

HENRY IV PART 2, 5.3.45

'LONDON IS ... so superior to other English towns that London is said not to be in England, but rather England to be in London' noted Thomas Platter, a visitor to the city in 1599. Although much smaller than today, regional migration and immigration swelled the population. In the late 1580s, when Shakespeare moved from his native Warwickshire to London, he was moving not only to the capital of the nation, but to the gateway to the world.

The river Thames brought the wealth and traffic of the world into the city. The historian William Camden wrote of the Thames: 'A man would say, that, seeth the shipping there, that it is, as it were, a very wood of trees disbranched to make glades and let in light, so shaded it is with masts and sails.' Shakespeare arrived in London at a time of growing national confidence as new companies traded with an expanding range of global contacts. The adventurer Sir Francis Drake was the second person to circumnavigate the globe between 1577 and 1581, however it was in an artificial globe, Shakespeare's playhouse at Bankside, that Londoners explored the strangeness and variety of humankind. Viewed from the London playhouse, all the world was a stage, and the stage was all the world.

Salisbury h.   New Exchange   Convent garden   S. Clement

Savoy   Somerset h.   Arundel house   Ghoe house   Temple stayres   Temple   Black fryars

Baynards

The Globe

Beere bayting h.

'Within this wooden O'

HENRY V, PROLOGUE.13

Here we see London viewed from the new suburb of Southwark, on the south bank of the Thames. This was the city's entertainment district. In 1599 the Globe theatre opened there, possibly with Shakespeare's *Julius Caesar*. The image shows the second Globe theatre built on the same site, mistakenly labelled as the 'Beere bayting house'. Bear baiting rivalled the playhouse as a popular attraction. This bear skull was found on the site of the Bear Garden, near the modern Globe. The violence of the bear fight is recalled in *Macbeth* as he is surrounded by his killers.

SKULL OF A BROWN BEAR
Excavated from the site
of the Globe Theatre in 1989
H 13.5 cm, W 20 cm, L 32 cm
Dulwich College, London

'bear-like I must fight the course'

MACBETH, 5.7.2

THE LONG VIEW (DETAIL)
Wenceslaus Hollar, Amsterdam, 1647
Etching on paper, H 46.6 cm, W 39 cm
British Museum, London

'My naked weapon is out. Quarrel, I will back thee'

ROMEO AND JULIET, 1.1.27

**RAPIER AND DAGGER FOUND
ON THE THAMES FORESHORE**
Rapier: late 1500s. Steel, wood
and copper alloy wire, L 128 cm
Dagger: *c.* 1600. Steel, wood and iron
wire, L 46.3 cm
Royal Armouries, Leeds

To get to Bankside you walked over London Bridge, underneath the heads of executed traitors displayed on spikes, or crossed the river by ferry. This image from a tourist album shows a recognizable London scene: well-dressed people being rowed over the Thames. Gentlemen and nobles wore a rapier and dagger as status symbols and for defence. These examples were found on the Thames foreshore. Public brawls were common, often involving actors and playwrights, and this violence was represented on stage. *Romeo and Juliet* is Shakespeare's tragedy of Elizabethan knife crime, which opens with rival noble factions fighting in the street.

GOING TO BANKSIDE
From the *Album Amicorum*
of Michael van Meer, *c.* 1619.
Pen and ink with watercolour
and gold highlighting on paper,
H 8 cm, W 16.7 cm
Edinburgh University Library, Edinburgh

Criminals were active in and around the theatres. This pamphlet describes them and their victims, known as 'conies' or rabbits. The crowded playhouse was an ideal site for pickpockets, since people brought money and fashionable accessories in with them. This fork, engraved with the owner's initials, is designed for sweetmeats and was found on the site of the Rose theatre. Hamlet refers to people standing in front of the stage as 'groundlings': a kind of fish found on the bottom of rivers, which looks up to the surface with its mouth open.

'to split the ears of the groundlings'

HAMLET, 3.2.7

FORK FROM THE ROSE
THEATRE WITH DETAIL
SHOWING OWNERSHIP
INSCRIPTION
1587–1606. Brass-topped iron, L 22.1 cm
Museum of London, London

*THE GROUNDWORKE
OF CONNY-CATCHING*
Anonymous author after
Thomas Harman, London, 1592
Page from printed book,
H 18.5 cm, W 14.5 cm
British Library, London

The burning of Maiſter Iohn Rogers, vicar of Saint Pulchers, and Reader of Paules in London.

ILLUSTRATION FROM JOHN FOXE'S *ACTS AND MONUMENTS* (OR *BOOK OF MARTYRS*)
Sixteenth-century edition
Woodcut, H 12.6 cm, W 17.4 cm
British Museum, London

'You are they
That made the air unwholesome when you cast
Your stinking greasy caps in hooting at
Coriolanus' exile.'

CORIOLANUS, 4.6.157–60

Public executions, unlike the theatres, offered free entertainment. This book illustration shows the execution of a Protestant martyr, John Rogers, which took place in 1554. Men in the crowd are wearing woollen caps, which in 1571 were legally prescribed for holiday wear. This example was found in Moorfields in London. Shakespeare refers to 'plain statute-caps' in *Love's Labour's Lost* and they were worn by groundlings at the playhouse. Shakespeare associates them with mass unrest in his Roman play *Coriolanus*.

WOOLLEN CAP
England, mid-1500s. Wool, knitted and felted, with silk. Diam. 24 cm
British Museum, London

Romance and reality

'now am I in Arden'

AS YOU LIKE IT, 2.4.10

S HAKESPEARE'S lifetime saw a new interest in mapping England and its counties. Christopher Saxton's survey of England and Wales in 1579 meant that, for the first time, educated English people could see how their locality related to others. This new sense of regional and national consciousness found expression in Shakespeare's plays. His Warwickshire origins were extremely important to him and his work throughout his life, and the plays are steeped in references to midland places, customs and folklore. His concept of rural England still persists today. Close observation of nature and an increasing interest in horticulture was widespread in Elizabethan society and this too was taken up at the London playhouse.

Shakespeare was born into an England that had separated itself from Catholic Europe. Elizabeth I's religious settlement of 1559 was a compromise, reaffirming Protestantism as the state religion and her status as Supreme Governor of the Church. Church worship was simplified; images were destroyed and old customs questioned. Shakespeare refers to ruined monasteries, and he explores with his audiences the sense of Catholicism as a lost faith, of the shattering of its sacred places and objects. He guarded his own beliefs, but his plays resonate with the controversies of the time.

'Wast born i'th'forest here?'

AS YOU LIKE IT, 5.1.17

This map, woven in tapestry around 1588, shows Shakespeare's native county of Warwickshire, including his home town of Stratford-upon-Avon. The detail shows the church of Holy Trinity in which the playwright was baptized and buried. Inside the church, and certainly known to Shakespeare, are some carved seats – misericords – made for the clergy in the 1400s. One of them shows the story of a 'scold': from a woman accused of being loud-mouthed or scurrilous in her community, to being bridled.

MISERICORD FROM
HOLY TRINITY CHURCH
SHOWING A 'SCOLD'
1400s. Carved wood
Holy Trinity Church,
Stratford-Upon-Avon

'SHELDON' TAPESTRY MAP
OF WARWICKSHIRE
(detail showing Stratford-upon-Avon)
Probably made in the Sheldon
tapestry workshop at Barcheston,
Warwickshire, c. 1588
Wool and silk, approx.
H 395 cm, W 520 cm
Warwickshire Museum Service,
Warwick

AVSTON

GOL

STRETFORD

CLIF

BISHOPTON

**POT WITH A PORTRAIT
OF A MELANCHOLY LOVER**
Probably made in Southwark, *c*. 1620
Tin-glazed earthenware, H 32.2 cm
Victoria and Albert Museum, London

**PORTRAIT MINIATURE OF
EDWARD HERBERT, 1ST BARON
HERBERT OF CHERBURY**
Isaac Oliver, *c*. 1613–14.
Vellum on card, H 18.1 cm, W 22.7 cm
Powis Castle, Powys

'it is a melancholy of mine own'

AS YOU LIKE IT, 4.1.11–12

Shakespeare explores and makes fun of the fashionable concept
of melancholy. Here, the poet philosopher Lord Herbert of
Cherbury lies in a forest glade. The evocation of landscape is new
in English art, and finds its parallel in Shakespeare's plays and
the poetry of Edmund Spenser. This type of imagery was seen as
particularly English and courtly, but the ceramic jug above shows
that it had a wider social reach. Here we see a melancholy young man
pining for his love: 'I AM NO BEGGAR I CAN NOT CRAVE
BUT YU KNOW THE THING THAT I WOULD HAVE.'

EMBROIDERED JACKET, DETAIL
English, 1600–25
Linen, hand-sewn and embroidered with silk, silver and silver-gilt thread,
L 66.5 cm
Victoria and Albert Museum, London

GILLYFLOWER AND PRIVET HAWK MOTH
Jacques Le Moyne, from an album c. 1585
Watercolour and bodycolour,
H 21.5 cm, W 14.5 cm
British Museum, London

'carnations and streaked gillyvors, Which some call nature's bastards'

THE WINTER'S TALE, 4.4.93–4

Shakespeare is said to have been a keen gardener. The destruction of the great monastic gardens at the Reformation led to developments in gardening practice and awareness in a wider population in England. Shakespeare's eye for flowers parallels the exquisite drawings of his contemporary Jacques Le Moyne, like this one of a gillyflower, a prized garden plant. Perdita in *The Winter's Tale* prefers simple flowers to hybrids like gillyflowers. Le Moyne also produced a pattern book of flower motifs for embroidery in 1586. The embroidered design on the jacket – perhaps for a pregnant woman – follows such models. Strawberries, peapods, acorns and honeysuckle evoke fertility and the contemporary English garden.

'Bare ruined choirs, where late the sweet birds sang'

SONNET 73, 4

The Elizabethan religious settlement of 1559 simplified church worship. The injunctions of that year demanded the destruction of the outward forms of Catholic worship, 'so that there remained no memory of the same'. The assault on custom is shown in this salt cellar made for secular use out of fragments of Catholic church plate or reliquaries destroyed at the Reformation. However, the ceremony of the Eucharist remained central to religious worship. The Protestant communion cup shown opposite was made to the new, prescribed form in 1571–2 for Bishopton chapel, close to Shakespeare's family church.

THE STONYHURST SALT
John Robinson (?), London, 1577–8
Silver-gilt, rock crystal, rubies
and garnets, H 26.2 cm
British Museum, London

BISHOPTON CUP

Robert Durrant, London, 1571–2
Silver, (cup) H 12.7 cm, Diam. of bowl
7.2 cm; (lid) H 3.3cm, Diam. 7.6 cm
Holy Trinity Church, Stratford-upon-Avon

'Come to the pedlar'

Catholic priests were the ultimate outsiders in Shakespeare's England. Living in concealment, they were often forced to travel in disguise as pedlars. Pedlars were familiar figures, with well-known routes along unpoliced tracks that formed a network through remote rural England. This is a pedlar's chest of *c.* 1600, but instead of stolen sheets like that of the pedlar Autolycus in *The Winter's Tale*, it contains items for celebrating the Catholic mass in secret, including a rosary (below), and priest's vestments made from women's clothing. The chest was hidden in a well-known Catholic safe house near Preston in Lancashire, and used by generations of Jesuit priests.

**PEDLAR'S CHEST
FOUND AT SAMLESBURY HALL,
NEAR PRESTON, LANCASHIRE**
Lancashire, *c.* 1600–30
Box, softwood covered with pony skin
and lined with printed paper, L 85 cm,
W 37 cm, H (closed) 34.5 cm
Stonyhurst College, Lancashire

BRACELET ROSARY
Found in the pedlar's chest (left)
Chalcedony, agate, steel chain,
L 10.2 cm
Stonyhurst College, Lancashire

The English past

'Cry, 'God for Harry, England,
and Saint George!"

HENRY V, 3.1.34

THE IMPORTANCE of the past and its lessons for the present were instilled at an early age in Shakespeare's England. Shakespeare made his name as the author of medieval history plays: both he and the playhouse played an important role in shaping national identity at a time when England was redefining herself as a Protestant state. In his series of plays about the shaping of England under the Tudor dynasty, Shakespeare maps the medieval past onto the present. Richard III, who was defeated by the first Tudor king Henry VII in 1485, is presented as the infamous 'Crookback'; Henry V as the ultimate patriotic warrior king.

Shakespeare's Roman history plays reflect the contemporary fascination with the classical world and debates over its legacy. The very real fear of conspiracy and assassination at the end of Elizabeth's reign, with no openly-acknowledged successor, raised the question: would England survive? These were censored issues, but setting them in the classical past in the public arena of the playhouse allowed them to be aired. In *Julius Caesar* Shakespeare sets the most famous assassination in history in a world redolent with contemporary national concerns.

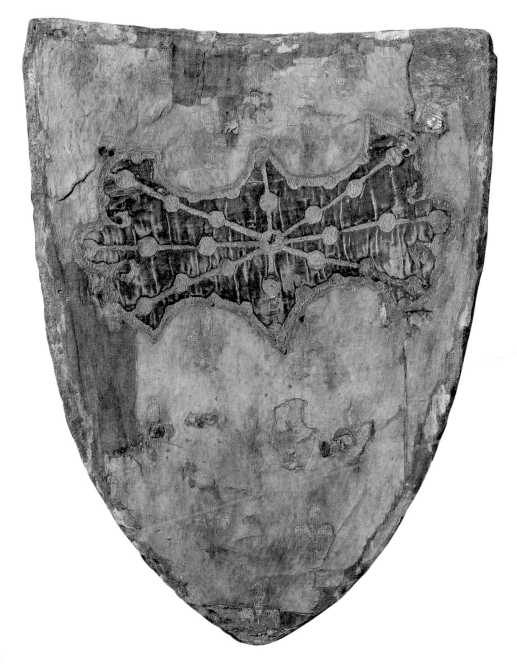

'bruisèd helmet and his bended sword'

HENRY V, 5.CHORUS.18

In *Henry V*, Shakespeare uses England's medieval past to stage a profound debate on the nature and conduct of war. Shakespeare refers to Henry's 'bruisèd helmet' and 'bended sword': arms and armour associated with Henry V were on display above his tomb in Westminster Abbey, and were on the tourist trail in London at the time. They made a fine display evoking the warrior king, and their presence in the Abbey suggests how objects, as well as texts, informed the image of the past.

**FUNERAL ACHIEVEMENTS
OF HENRY V**
Shield: probably late 1300s. Limewood and textile, H 61 cm, W 39.4 cm
Helmet: early 1400s. Iron or steel and copper alloy, H 42.5 cm, W 25.4 cm, Diam. 32.4 cm
Sword: 1400s or 1500s. Steel, iron and wood, L 89.5 cm, of blade 73 cm
Westminster Abbey, London

'And every tale condemns me for a villain.'

RICHARD III, 5.3.199

Richard III was portrayed by the Tudors as a deformed, villainous ruler. This portrait presents that stereotype, showing Richard with a broken sword symbolizing broken kingship, with a raised left shoulder and a withered hand. The boar was used by Richard as his own heraldic device, and the resonance of his identification with this savage beast was one with a particular political meaning for Shakespeare's audiences.

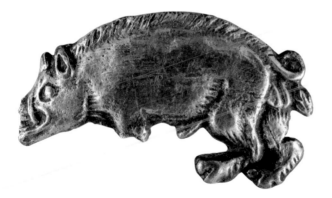

**RICHARD III WITH
A BROKEN SWORD**
Unknown artist, mid-1500s
Oil on oak panel, H 48.5 cm, W 35.5 cm
Society of Antiquaries, London

LIVERY BADGE
In the shape of a boar, *c.* 1470–85
Silver-gilt, L 3.2 cm, W 2.35 cm
British Museum, London

THE LIFE OF
Marcus Brutus.

A M Arcus Brutus came of that *Iunius Brutus*, for whome the auncient Romanes made his statue of brasse to be set vp in the Capitoll, with the
images of the kings, holding a naked sword in his hand: bicause he had
valliantly put downe the Tarqvines from their kingdom of Rome.
But that *Iunius Brutus* being of a sower stearne nature, not softned by
reason, being like vnto sword blades of too hard a temper: was so sub-
iect to his choller and malice he bare vnto the tyrannes, that for their
sakes he caused his owne sonnes to be executed. But this *Marcus Bru-*
tus in contrarie maner, whose life we presently wryte, hauing framed
his manners of life by the rules of vertue and studie of Philosophie, and hauing imployed his

The parētage of Brutus.

Brutus ma-ners.

B wit, which was gentle and constant, in attempting of great things: me thinkes he was rightly
made and framed vnto vertue. So that his verie enemies which wish him most hurt, bicause
of his conspiracy against *Iulius Cæsar*: if there were any noble attempt done in all this conspi-
racie, they referre it whollie vnto *Brutus*, and all the cruell and violent actes vnto *Cassius*, who

Seruilia M

'Beware the Ides of March'

JULIUS CAESAR, 1.2.21

AUREUS OF MARCUS JUNIUS BRUTUS
43–2 BC. Gold, Diam. 2.01 cm
British Museum, London

'LIFE OF BRUTUS', FROM PLUTARCH'S
THE LIVES OF THE NOBLE GRECIANS AND ROMANES
Translated by Thomas North, London, 1579
Printed book, open at page 1055
British Library, London

Ancient Rome is projected onto Tudor London in Shakespeare's Roman history plays. Fear of conspiracy and assassination overshadowed England in the 1590s. All educated men and women in Elizabethan England knew the story of Julius Caesar's murder in 44 BC. This coin, minted by Brutus in 43–2 BC, commemorates the date of the murder: the fifteenth – or 'Ides' – of March. Roman coins were known and collected in Shakespeare's England as historical evidence, but Shakespeare's main source for the play was Plutarch's *Lives of the Noble Grecians and Romanes*, translated by Thomas North in 1579.

**CAMEO: THE SUICIDE
OF CLEOPATRA**
Late 1500s, North Italy
Sardonyx, engraved, H 3.5 cm, W 2 cm
British Museum, London

'The stroke of death is as a lover's pinch Which hurts and is desired.'

ANTONY AND CLEOPATRA, 5.2.331–2

The most famous suicide in history was that of the ancient Egyptian queen Cleopatra, who chose death rather than dishonour after a spectacular love affair with the Roman general Mark Antony. This was a loaded subject in Elizabethan England, given the queen's passion for her general, the Earl of Essex. The two queens feature in these playing cards (opposite), as female rulers in overwhelmingly masculine worlds. Cleopatra's suicide was part of the visual culture of Shakespeare's Europe: both the cameo (above) and the playing card show her with the asp, moments before she is killed by its venom.

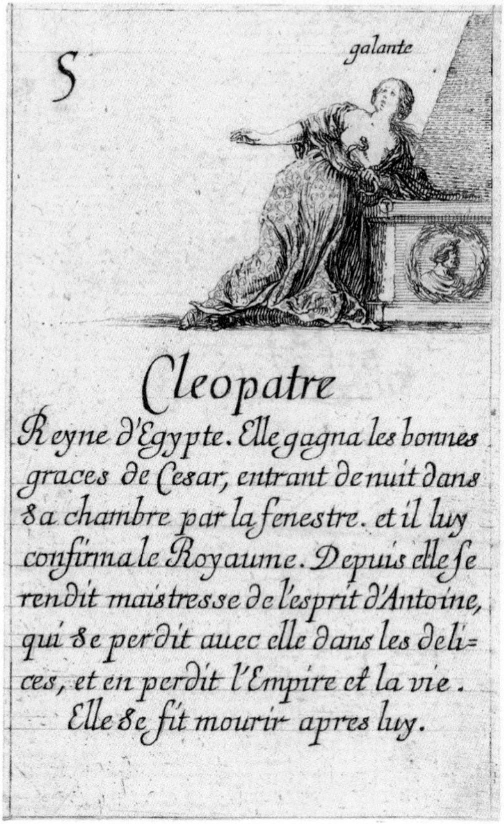

**PLAYING CARDS OF ELIZABETH
AND CLEOPATRA**
Stefano della Bella, 1644
Etchings, Elizabeth H 8.9 cm W 5.5 cm;
Cleopatra H 8.7 cm, W 5.5 cm
British Museum, London

'And the imperial votress passèd on,
In maiden meditation, fancy-free'

A MIDSUMMER NIGHT'S DREAM, 2.1.166–7

The jewel above compares Elizabeth, portrayed on one side, with the legendary phoenix on the other. The phoenix, which rose out of its own ashes to live once more, was an emblem of chastity. Shakespeare uses the image in his poem 'The Phoenix and the Turtle'. As an unmarried virgin queen Elizabeth identified herself with the virtue of chastity to her English subjects. In the portrait shown opposite she is seen as a 'fair vestal' of Ancient Rome, Tuccia, who carried water from the Tiber in a sieve to prove her virginity. The painting suggests Elizabeth's lineage from ancient Trojan heroes in the column on the left, while the globe on the right indicates imperial ambition in the New World.

PENDANT MEDALLION:
THE PHOENIX JEWEL
England, *c.* 1570–80
Gold medal surrounded by a border wreath of enamel flowers, H (incl. suspension loop) 6.1 cm, W 4.6 cm
British Museum, London

QUEEN ELIZABETH I IN THE GUISE OF THE VESTAL VIRGIN TUCCIA (*THE SIEVE PORTRAIT*)
Quentin Metsys the Younger, 1583
Oil on canvas, H 124.5 cm, W 91.5 cm
Pinacoteca Nazionale, Siena

The British future

'His honour and the greatness of his name
Shall be, and make new nations'

HENRY VIII, 5.4.55–6

FOLLOWING THE death of Elizabeth I in 1603, James VI of Scotland was welcomed as James I of England. James' accession created a new international entity, 'Great Britain', and it represented a fresh start after decades of tension and division. Catholic hopes of toleration turned sour in the Gunpowder Plot of 1605. Catholic priests executed for their alleged role in the Plot were condemned as witches. James perceived witchcraft as a political crime, which he had experienced personally.

Shakespeare's relationship with the court changed in 1603, when his acting company was renamed 'The King's Men'. *Macbeth* is steeped in the new king's preoccupations: the relationship between Scotland and England, succession and legitimacy, conspiracy and witchcraft.

James's vision for 'Great Britain' questioned British history and origins. Did civil society originate with the Romans? Could a modern British empire 'civilize' the Algonquian Indians of America, and the Gaels of Scotland?

In his medieval histories of the 1590s, Shakespeare referred to his country as England. But when he wrote *Cymbeline* in 1610, he used the words 'Britain' or 'Britains' nearly fifty times. A fantasy about ancient Britain ends with a peace evoking James I's treaty with Spain in 1604. The mood is one of promise.

'dire combustion and confused events'

MACBETH, 2.3.52

'GUY FAWKES' LANTERN'
Early 1600s. Sheet iron, H 34.5 cm
Ashmolean Museum, Oxford

The Gunpowder Plot of 1605 was a Catholic terrorist attempt
to blow up James I, his family, parliament, and the judiciary.
The aim was to establish a new Catholic government. The lantern
is thought to have been taken from terrorists caught in the act,
while the contemporary print shows and names some of the
conspirators and the manner of their execution. The event provides
the essential backdrop for Shakespeare's *Macbeth*, which deals with
'dire combustion and confused events'. It is in this play that
Shakespeare introduces the word 'assassination' into English
literature. Commemorated annually on 5 November, Guy Fawkes
Night, the plot has become part of the British national imagination.

'Out, vile jelly!
Where is thy lustre now?'

KING LEAR, 3.7.88–9

This is a reliquary made to contain the eyeball of the Jesuit priest Edward Oldcorne, who was executed in 1606 for his perceived role in the Gunpowder Plot. As a traitor he was hanged, drawn and quartered; part of the 'theatre of punishment', which competed with the playhouse as popular spectacle. The Duke of Cornwall's relish in plucking out Gloucester's eyes in *King Lear* owes its force to the experience of public execution. Visscher's drawing opposite of the execution of eight plotters on 31 January 1606 makes the details real enough. Oldcorne's eye was illegally gathered by a Catholic bystander at his execution and kept as a relic.

RELIQUARY CONTAINING THE RIGHT EYE OF BLESSED EDWARD OLDCORNE SJ
c. 1606. Silver, Diam. 4.6 cm
Stonyhurst College, Lancashire

STUDY FOR A PRINT DEPICTING THE EXECUTION OF CONSPIRATORS IN THE GUNPOWDER PLOT
Claes Jansz Visscher, *c.* 1606
Pen and brown ink, brown wash, with lines indented for transfer, H 23.9 cm, W 34.2 cm
British Museum, London

'Though his bark cannot be lost,
Yet it shall be tempest-tossed'

MACBETH, 1.3.25–6

CHURCH SHIP
Denmark (?), c. 1589
Wood, H 65 cm, L 64.5 cm
National Museums Scotland, Edinburgh

James VI's marriage to Anne of Denmark in 1590 was threatened by terrible storms, which were thought to be the work of witches. James believed he had survived owing to divine protection. The model ship (opposite) is a votive or thanksgiving for his safe return home. It is said to have hung in the kirk (church) at South Leith, the port for Edinburgh. James tried the accused at the North Berwick witch trials of 1590, publicized in *Newes from Scotland* in 1591: this woodcut shows the witches cooking up the storm in their cauldron. James' experience and details of the witches' statements appear to have informed Shakespeare's *Macbeth*.

NEWES FROM SCOTLAND
London, 1591(?)
Woodcut, H 18.7 cm, 13.4 cm
Bodleian Library, Oxford

Magical thinking was universal in Shakespeare's world. Witchcraft was a crime. The iron collar (jougs, below right) from Fife was used on suspected criminals, including witches, as was the Scottish bridle (branks, above right), which gagged and chained a woman in a public place. Shakespeare's weyard sisters in *Macbeth* touch briefly on the witches of European tradition: one of them talks of 'killing swine'. The witch's cursing bone from Ayrshire (opposite), used to curse livestock, is an amuletic charm, which demonstrates the force of witchcraft in Scottish culture. Shakespeare's witches are mysterious female prophets, but their hypnotic charms are deeply rooted in contemporary British folklore.

'If you prick us, do we not bleed?'

THE MERCHANT OF VENICE, 3.1.44

WITCH'S BRIDLE (BRANKS)
AND IRON COLLAR (JOUGS)
Scotland, 1600s
Iron, branks H. 19.2 cm;
jougs H 9 cm; Diam. 15.5 cm
National Museums Scotland, Edinburgh

'killing swine'

MACBETH, 1.3.2

WITCH'S CURSING BONE
Glen Shira, Inveraray, Argyll,
possibly 1800s
Deer or sheep's thigh bone
and bog oak, H 11 cm, W 7 cm
National Museums Scotland, Edinburgh

'shall Banquo's issue ever Reign in this kingdom?'

MACBETH, 4.1.110–1

James I was insecure about his legitimacy as king of England. The *Lyte Jewel* (above) was given by James I, very publicly at Whitehall Palace, to Thomas Lyte in 1610 in gratitude for a royal genealogy justifying his claim to the throne (opposite). The genealogy traced James's descent from Brutus, mythical Trojan founder of the British nation. The story of James' decent from Banquo and Fleance lies behind Shakespeare's *Macbeth*, in which it is Banquo's line, not Macbeth's, which will produce future kings of Scotland, culminating in James himself.

In my poore opinion this wyll be the most fytest
for this is lyke men and to out thenceth on to other

Effingham

'the British crown'

CYMBELINE, 3.5.78

At his accession in 1603, James I of England
and VI of Scotland ruled over a new international
entity: 'Great Britain'. James dreamed of full
union between England and Scotland and he
explored the possibility of a new British flag
(opposite), joining the cross of St George
(England) with that of St Andrew (Scotland).
The chosen design gives parity to the two nations.
James used his coinage to promote union. This
gold sovereign (right) was known as the 'unite'
and proclaims James 'King of Great Britain'.
Shakespeare echoes James's aims in his play,
Cymbeline.

**DESIGNS FOR THE UNION FLAG
OF GREAT BRITAIN**
c. 1604. Watercolour, pen and ink on
paper, H 29 cm, W 43 cm
National Library of Scotland, Edinburgh

UNITE COIN OF JAMES I
Minted in England, 1612–13
Gold, Diam. 3.8 cm
British Museum, London

THE SOMERSET HOUSE CONFERENCE
Unknown artist, *c.* 1604
Oil on canvas, H 205.7 cm, W 268 cm
National Portrait Gallery, London

'Publish we this peace To all our subjects'

CYMBELINE, 5.4.562–3

In 1604 James negotiated peace between Spain, the most powerful European Christian empire, and Britain. It was a propaganda coup after decades of war. The painting opposite commemorates the signing of the treaty in London at which a splendid medieval gold cup was given by James I to the Spanish as a peace pledge (right). The cup played an acknowledged role in the making of modern history, and Shakespeare, as a King's Man, may have witnessed its ceremonial presentation. Shakespeare's *Cymbeline* evokes ancient Britain as a satellite state to Rome, and it ends with a peace comparable to that negotiated in 1604.

THE ROYAL GOLD CUP
Paris, *c.* 1370–80, with later alterations
Gold with enamel and pearls, H (with cover) 23.6 cm, Diam. of cup 17.8 cm
British Museum, London

'Cymbeline King of Britain'

CYMBELINE, TITLE

James I's plans for the future of 'Great Britain' demanded a new history for the origins of the British people. In *Cymbeline* Shakespeare presents a fantasy about ancient Britain and its relationship with the Roman empire. Little was known about the historical Cunobelin, the Cymbeline of his play. William Camden was the first to look at coins as evidence for Roman Britain: engraved coin plates appear in the English edition of his book of 1610 on the history of Britain (opposite). One of these shows a coin (stater) of Cunobelin (above), with a rearing classical horse and a wheat ear with Latin inscriptions, suggesting that he was a powerful king in a Southern Britain close to Rome.

GOLD STATER OF CUNOBELIN
Minted in the North Thames or Kent area and found at Weston, Northamptonshire, c. AD 10–40
Gold, Diam. 1.8 cm
British Museum, London

BRITAIN, OR
A CHOROGRAPHICALL DESCRIPTION OF THE MOST FLOURISHING KINGDOMES, ENGLAND, SCOTLAND, AND IRELAND
William Camden, London, 1610
Open at page 89, H 34 cm, W 24 cm
British Library, London

Nummi Britannici antiqui.

'Made Lud's town with rejoicing fires bright, And Britons strut with courage'

CYMBELINE, 3.1.35–6

Finding a new history for ancient Britain raised questions about the native British tribes that the Romans had overcome at their invasion. Did civil society in Britain originate with the Romans? Was there a parallel with the English colonization attempt in America? Like the Algonquian Indians encountered by the English in Virginia (right), ancient Britons had painted their bodies. John White presents a warlike, painted pict (opposite) brandishing his enemy's head, an image evoked by the queen in Shakespeare's *Cymbeline*. If the picts had been civilized by the Romans, could not a modern British empire 'civilize' the Algonquian Indians of America, the wild Irish and the Gaels of Scotland?

**A PICTISH WARRIOR
HOLDING A HUMAN HEAD**
John White, 1585–93
Watercolour and bodycolour over
graphite, touched with pen and ink,
H 24.3 cm, W 16.9 cm
British Museum, London

**AN INDIAN WEROWANCE, OR
CHIEF, PAINTED FOR A GREAT
SOLEMN GATHERING**
John White, 1585–93
Watercolour over graphite, touched with
bodycolour, white (altered) and gold,
H 26.3 cm, W 15 cm
British Museum, London

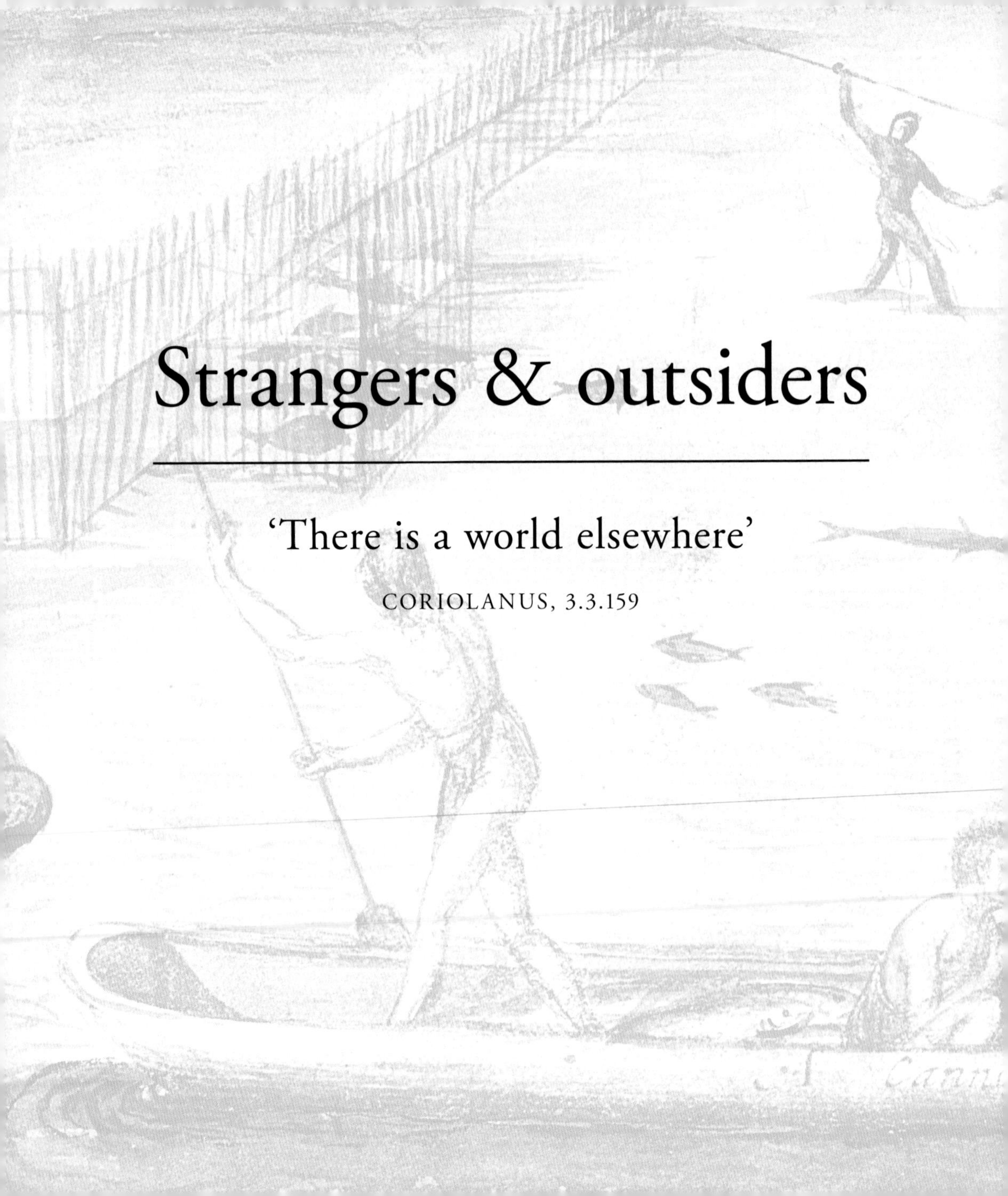

Strangers & outsiders

'There is a world elsewhere'

CORIOLANUS, 3.3.159

S HAKESPEARE'S culture was European, and as far as we know he never left England, yet his places of imagination extended across the known world. The global conversation was taken up in the playhouse, which played a key role in the imagining of outsiders.

Venice had a special hold on the English as a fashionable city with a multicultural population. It was also a culture to criticize, and by defining what was foreign or alien the English, then the British, began to know themselves as a nation.

Venice was a proxy setting for London in the playhouse and was perceived as a centre of luxury and licence, notorious for its beautiful women of questionable morals. It is in the Venetian plays that Shakespeare explores religious and racial identity by examining the status of 'strangers': immigrants, aliens and outsiders.

Shakespeare's Britain had a rapidly expanding range of global contacts. His last solo-authored play, *The Tempest*, presents debates about the nature of sovereignty, plantation and colonization that resonate today. Its New World aura reveals the wonder of the early literature of travel and exploration for British audiences.

'Bring them, I pray thee with imagined speed Unto the traject, to the common ferry Which trades to Venice'

THE MERCHANT OF VENICE, 3.4.53-5

Shakespeare used the city of Venice to tackle issues of concern for his audiences. In Venice, Londoners pictured their own desires and fears: their own future. This painting presents a panorama of Venice as the ultimate modern city, as Shakespeare and his audiences imagined it. The detail opposite shows people crossing the Grand Canal by ferry (*traghetto*). In *The Merchant of Venice* Shakespeare makes a confused reference to *traghetti*.

BIRD'S-EYE VIEW OF VENICE
Odoardo Fialetti, 1611
Oil on canvas, H 215.9 cm, W 424.2 cm
Eton College, Berkshire

Venice was famous for luxury. The glass opposite presents the picture-postcard stereotype of the tempting Venetian beauty, complete with horned hairstyle and desirable accessories: an ostrich-feather fan and handkerchief. The miniature from a Scottish tourist album (below) shows such a woman, whose scandalous underclothes – breeches and platform shoes – are uncovered when you lift the flap of her dress. She is then revealed as a courtesan. This preoccupation with the virtue of women is a major theme in Shakespeare's Venetian-set plays.

'I fear me it will make me scandalized.'

THE TWO GENTLEMEN OF VERONA, 2.7.61

'In Venice they do let heaven see the pranks
They dare not show their husbands'

OTHELLO, 3.3.225–6

**GOBLET WITH
WOMAN AND FAN**
Venice or Northern Europe, *c.* 1600
Blown glass, enamelled and gilded,
H 21.5 cm, Diam. 12.6 cm
British Museum, London

**MINIATURE OF A VENETIAN
COURTESAN**
From the friendship album of
Sir Michael Balfour, 1596–9
Open at f. 128r.
Album, H 16 cm, W 25 cm
National Library of Scotland, Edinburgh

'noble Moor'

OTHELLO, 3.4.20

'were't to renounce his baptism'

OTHELLO, 2.3.307

The portrait opposite presents an unidentified sub-Saharan African as a Christian courtier, perhaps hinting at the emergence of a new European black identity. His silver hat-badge records a visit to a famous Belgian shrine, the black Madonna at Hal. But was he a visiting sub-Saharan dignitary, or a courtier born in Europe? Shakespeare's Venetian plays question religious and racial identity in a period of global expansion. *Othello* is trusted by the Venetian state as a general on the front line, but he is a baptized Moor whose allegiance and identity is uncertain in Christian society. Through the imagining of outsiders, 'strangers', the British came to understand themselves.

PILGRIM BADGE OF THE MADONNA OF HAL
Belgium or the Netherlands, early 1500s
Silver gilt, embossed and pierced,
Diam. 3.8 cm
British Museum, London

PORTRAIT OF AN AFRICAN MAN
Jan Jansz Mostaert, *c.* 1525–30
Oil on panel, H 30.8 cm, W 21.2 cm
Rijksmuseum, Amsterdam

'far more fair than black'

OTHELLO, 1.3.308

Many of the black Africans in Shakespeare's London, as in other European cities, were servants. The fire-blower (right) of around 1500, in the form of a head of a young sub-Saharan African, presents the common visual stereotype. The marble bust of a black African (opposite), made in Rome around 1610, suggests a developing aesthetic of blackness in European sculpture, which owed something, however misunderstood or manipulated, to the actual encounter with Africa and Africans in Europe. Their arrival shaped language itself: 'black' and 'white' came into common linguistic use with reference to skin colour from the 1400s. In the language of Shakespeare's *Othello*, the patterning of black against white explores whiteness by contrast.

BUST OF A BLACK AFRICAN
Nicholas Cordier, *c.* 1610
Black *bigio morato* marble and
white marble, H. 34 cm
Staatliche Kunstsammlungen, Dresden

**FIRE-BLOWER IN THE FORM OF
THE BUST OF A BLACK AFRICAN**
Venice, *c.* 1500
Embossed sheet copper with traces
of patination and gilding, H 25.4 cm
British Museum, London

'Had I plantation of this isle'

THE TEMPEST, 2.1.131

The idea that England had an empire, beyond rebellious Ireland, during the reign of Elizabeth I has little claim to reality. One ambition was to pacify the south west of Ireland, in the Munster plantation of 1586. The design opposite for the Great Seal of Ireland dates from just before the first English attempts to colonize Virginia in North America. The seal-die below of 1584 names Sir Walter Ralegh as 'lord and Governor' of Roanoke, Virginia; exactly the kind of private fiefdom mocked in the *The Tempest*.

DESIGN FOR THE OBVERSE OF QUEEN ELIZABETH'S GREAT SEAL OF IRELAND
Nicholas Hilliard, *c.* 1584–5
Pen and black ink with grey wash over graphite on vellum,
Diam. approx. 12.4 cm
British Museum, London

SEAL-DIE OF SIR WALTER RALEGH AS GOVERNOR OF VIRGINIA
1584. Silver, Diam. 5.7 cm
British Museum, London

'when they will not give a doit to relieve a lame beggar, they will lay out ten to see a dead Indian'

THE TEMPEST, 2.2.27–8

London's global contacts were expanding through international trade, colonization and diplomacy in Shakespeare's lifetime. Living people were brought back to England as curiosities. This drawing shows Kalicho, an Inuk brought back from Baffin Island by Martin Frobisher in 1577. Even dead bodies of 'Indians' might be shown off for profit. Trinculo in Shakespeare's *Tempest* seems to refer to this callous practice when he thinks of exhibiting the native islander, Caliban, in London. He mentions ten doits (below) – a near worthless Dutch coin – as an entrance fee. The playhouse was the best place in which to explore such cultural encounters.

KALICHO, AN INUK FROM FROBISHER BAY
After John White, 1585–93
Watercolour, with pen and grey ink on paper, H 39 cm, W 26 cm
British Museum, London

DOIT
Minted in the Netherlands, early 1600s
Alloy, Diam. 2 cm
British Museum, London

The manner of their fishing.

'I'll fish for thee'

THE TEMPEST, 2.2.124

Caliban is a native of the island in *The Tempest*. When the shipwrecked Sebastian and Trinculo encounter him, they are quick to exchange alcohol for survival tips. Caliban's skills at fishing and hunting are those of the medieval 'wild man' of European imagination and demonstrate his oneness with the natural world. The Brazilian marmoset (below) is one of the play's few specific New World references, though John White's watercolour of native Virginians fishing (opposite) shows the kinds of dams on which the English colonists depended, and to which Caliban refers in the play. In imagining Caliban for British audiences, Shakespeare draws on both ancient and medieval mythology, and New World travel literature.

'how to snare the nimble marmoset'

THE TEMPEST, 2.2.129–30

**FOUR STUDIES
OF A MARMOSET**
Unknown artist, *c.* 1520–50
Pen and grey ink with watercolour
and bodycolour, heightened with white,
party silhouetted, H 39.6 cm, W 28 cm
British Museum, London

INDIANS FISHING
John White, 1585–93
Watercolour over graphite, touched
with bodycolour and gold,
H 35.3 cm, W 23.5 cm
British Museum, London

The island in *The Tempest* is the former domain of Caliban's mother: the witch Sycorax, banished from Algiers for witchcraft. Her name recalls Circe, the ancient enchantress of Homer and Ovid, who had famously turned Odysseus' men into swine. This Greek pot shows Circe as a black African offering Odysseus a drugged drink. Her loom is emblematic of feminine trickery. One of Odysseus' crew is shown turned into a swine. He is trapped within the enchantment, as the human Caliban is penned by Prospero, like a pig. In making Prospero's island a place of powerful enchantments, Shakespeare draws on ancient literature and myth in a way familiar to many in his audiences in the London playhouse.

BLACK-FIGURED SKYPHOS WITH CIRCE AND ODYSSEUS
Boeotia, Greece, 450–420 BC
Pottery, painted and incised,
H 19.05 cm, Diam. 19.05 cm
British Museum, London

'This damned witch Sycorax'

THE TEMPEST, 1.2.311

'here you sty me
In this hard rock'

THE TEMPEST, 1.2.400–1

'His tears run down his beard, like winter's drops From eaves of reeds'

THE TEMPEST, 5.1.18–9

Prospero as 'shaman' is a figure recognizable in many world cultures, as is often brought out in productions of the play. This Taíno figure of a male spirit-being, in a drug-induced trance, evokes aspects of Ariel's descriptions of the men that Prospero has frozen through his 'rough magic', even to the gilded tear channels. The sculpture expresses the universal nature of enchantment. In a rapidly expanding society, where New World encounters questioned Old World certainties, how were British audiences to understand this 'brave new world' that was opening up all around them?

FIGURE OF A MALE SPIRIT BEING
Taíno, Jamaica, 1400s–1500s
Guayacan wood, H 104 cm
British Museum, London

GVLIELMO SHAKSPEARE
ANNO POST MORTEM CXXIV
AMOR PVBLICVS PÓSVIT

WILLIAM SHAKESPEARE 1564~1616
BURIED AT STRATFORD-ON-AVON

Conclusion

THE FIRST DUKE OF MARLBOROUGH, the great general and politician (and ancestor of Winston Churchill), is supposed to have remarked that his knowledge of history was derived entirely from Shakespeare, just as his theology was confined to John Milton's poem *Paradise Lost*. A positive cult of Shakespeare grew through the decades of the eighteenth century, with the result that by the time of the Romantic movement and the Victorian era the playwright from Stratford-upon-Avon had become not just the embodiment of creative genius, but a national divinity.

The midland counties in the vicinity of his home town came to be thought of as the 'heart of England'. A passing reference to Robin Hood in *As You Like It*, together with the song 'Under the greenwood tree', was sufficient to associate Shakespeare with an imagined lost world of fierce fairness mixed with relaxed jollity. He became an icon of allegedly authentic Englishness. Shakespeare's versions of history entered deep into the popular imagination, partly as a result of the charismatic stage performances of actors such as David Garrick and Edmund Kean. Richard II as a weak king, Henry V as a heroic one, Richard III as the evil and deformed murderer of the princes in the tower: their real histories were all more complicated than this, as indeed are Shakespeare's

**MARBLE MEMORIAL TO
WILLIAM SHAKESPEARE
IN POET'S CORNER,
WESTMINSTER ABBEY**
Peter Scheemakers, 1741
Wesminster Abbey, London

representations of them, but it was the headline images from the plays that stuck. So too with the classical world: the conscience of Brutus and the sexual allure of Cleopatra were, thanks to Shakespeare, the things that everybody remembered.

By the same account, Hamlet became the archetype of the tortured individual, Falstaff of the fat and funny bon viveur, Romeo and Juliet of the young couple madly in love, Beatrice and Benedick of the mature lovers well-matched by their verbal sparring, Lady Macbeth of the woman driving her husband's ambition, Malvolio of the pompous spoilsport, and so on. More troublingly, sometimes prejudicial notions of blackness were projected onto Othello and of Jewishness onto Shylock.

With each new turn of history, Shakespeare seemed to have got there first. *The Tempest* was written at the earliest dawn of colonial endeavour, but as the British empire spread around the world, the play spoke eloquently of the psychology of imperialism. Then when empire came to an end in the second half of the twentieth century, writers born into subjection in the Caribbean, in Africa and India, found their own voices through the example of Caliban: 'Freedom, high-day! High-day, freedom! Freedom, high-day, freedom!' Shakespeare's works were a source of inspiration in every corner of the world, from Martinique, where liberation poet Aimé Césaire rewrote *The Tempest*, to Robben Island, where Nelson Mandela and his fellow prisoners annotated their favourite lines in a smuggled copy of the *Complete Works*.

The poet and dramatist Ben Jonson predicted that there would come a time when his friend and rival dramatist would be held in as high regard as the great writers of antiquity. 'Triumph, my Britain, thou hast one to show', he wrote, 'To whom all Scenes of Europe homage owe.' Shakespeare's Britain was a multifaceted place, emerging through the collision and combining of many different forces and circumstances. Britain's Shakespeare was a creation of the eighteenth and nineteenth centuries, an era during which the nation and thus the national poet moved on the world stage. There is, wrote Maurice Morgann, one of his eighteenth century admirers,

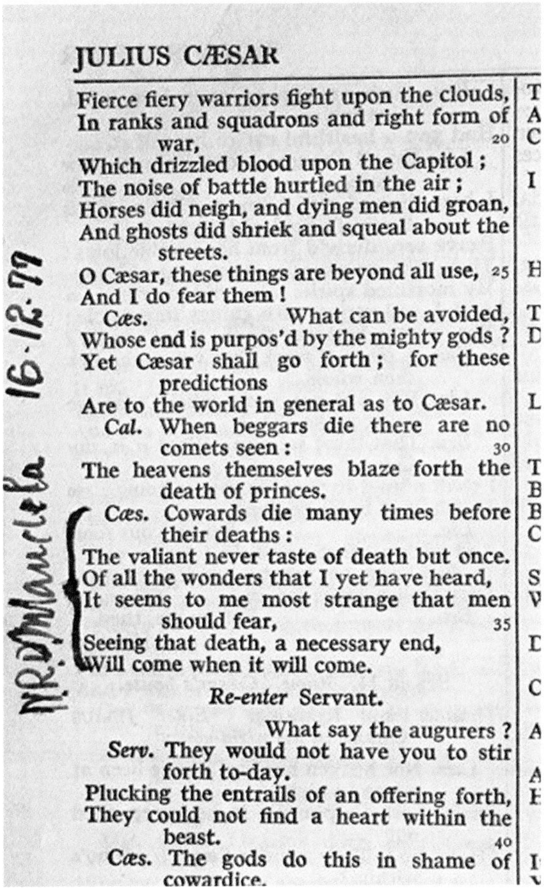

JULIUS CÆSAR

Fierce fiery warriors fight upon the clouds, | T
In ranks and squadrons and right form of | A
  war, 20 | C
Which drizzled blood upon the Capitol; |
The noise of battle hurtled in the air; | I
Horses did neigh, and dying men did groan, |
And ghosts did shriek and squeal about the |
  streets. |
O Cæsar, these things are beyond all use, 25 | H
And I do fear them! |
  Cæs.   What can be avoided, | T
Whose end is purpos'd by the mighty gods? | D
Yet Cæsar shall go forth; for these |
  predictions |
Are to the world in general as to Cæsar. | L
  Cal. When beggars die there are no |
    comets seen: 30 |
The heavens themselves blaze forth the | T
  death of princes. | B
  Cæs. Cowards die many times before | B
  their deaths: | C
The valiant never taste of death but once. |
Of all the wonders that I yet have heard, | S
It seems to me most strange that men | V
  should fear, 35 |
Seeing that death, a necessary end, | D
Will come when it will come. |

         Re-enter Servant. | C

         What say the augurers? | A
  Serv. They would not have you to stir |
  forth to-day. | A
Plucking the entrails of an offering forth, | E
They could not find a heart within the |
  beast. 40 |
  Cæs. The gods do this in shame of | I
  cowardice. |

Handwritten in margin: 16·12·77 ; NR Mandela

'nothing perishable about him … the Apalachian mountains, the
banks of the Ohio, and the plains of Sciota, shall resound with [his]
accents … when even the memory of the language in which he has
written shall be no more.' By the twentieth and twenty-first
centuries, it was not just 'all scenes of Europe', but almost all
countries in the world that paid homage to William Shakespeare.

Further reading

Jonathan Bate, *Soul of the Age*, London 2008

Julian Bowsher and Pat Miller, *The Rose and the Globe – Playhouses of Shakespeare's Bankside, Southwark, Excavations 1988–90*, London 2009

T.F. Earle and K.J.P. Lowe (eds), *Black Africans in Renaissance Europe*, Cambridge 2005

Mary Floyd-Wilson, *English Ethnicity and Race in Early Modern Drama*, Cambridge 2003

Antonia Fraser, *The Gunpowder Plot*, London 1996

Russell Fraser, *Young Shakespeare*, New York 1988

John Gillies, *Shakespeare and the Geography of Difference*, Cambridge 1994

Julian Goodare, Lauren Martin and Joyce Miller (eds),
Witchcraft and Belief in Early Modern Scotland, Basingstoke 2008

Imtiaz Habib, *Black Lives in the English Archives, 1500–1677: Imprints of the Invisible*, Aldershot 2008

Andrew Hadfield, *Shakespeare, Spenser and the Matter of Britain*, Basingstoke 2004

Peter Hulme and William B. Sherman (eds), '*The Tempest*' and its Travels, London 2000

James Shapiro, *1599: A Year in the Life of William Shakespeare*, London 2005

Kim Sloan, *A New World: England's First View of America*, exh. cat. British Museum, London 2007

Alden T. Vaughan and Virginia Mason Vaughan, *Shakespeare's Caliban: A Cultural History*, Cambridge 1991

Michael Wood, *In Search of Shakespeare*, London 2003

Image credits

Except where otherwise stated, photographs are © The Trustees of the British Museum. British Museum registration numbers are listed below. Further information about the Museum and its collection can be found at britishmuseum.org.

p. 1 and 27 By kind permission of Warwickshire Museum service, 2012

p. 2 and 30 The Trustees of the British Museum
(PD 1962,0714.1.18)

pp. 6–7 The Trustees of the British Museum
(PD 1880,1113.1126.1–4)

p. 9 The Trustees of the British Museum Donated by Sir Augustus Wollaston Franks
(CM 1882,0507.1)

p. 11 By permission of the Governors of Stonyhurst College

p. 12 National Museum of Wales

p. 16 The Trustees of the British Museum (PD 1864, 0611.434)

p. 17 © Dulwich College

p. 18 © Board of Trustees of the Armouries

p. 19 By courtesy of Edinburgh University Library, Special Collections Department

p. 20 © Museum of London

p. 21 © British Library Board

p. 22 The Trustees of the British Museum (PD 1877,0512.872)

p. 23 The Trustees of the British Museum (PE 1856, 0701.1882)

p. 26 © Inspired Images 2011. By kind permission of Holy Trinity Church, Stratford-upon-Avon

p. 28 The Right Honourable the Earl of Powis, Powis Castle, Powys. ©NTPL/John Hammond/by kind permission of the Powis Estate Trustees

p. 29 © Victoria and Albert Museum, London

p. 31 © Victoria and Albert Museum, London. Given by A. Solomon

p. 32 The Trustees of the British Museum. Purchased with assistance from The Art Fund (PE 1958,1004.1)

p. 33 © Inspired Images 2011. By kind permission of Holy Trinity Church, Stratford-upon-Avon

Acknowledgements

The authors would like to thank the following people
for their help and support in producing this book:

Claudia Bloch, John Cheal, Barrie Cook, Teresa Francis,
Martin Gorick, Jan Graffius, Melanie Morris, Axelle Russo,
Henrietta Ryan, Ann Thornton, Tony Trowles, Roland Walters,
Jeremy and William Warren, Will Webb, Sarah Williams,
Michael Winckless, Maggie Wood.